COMMANDER IN BEEF

Donald Gorbach

ISBN-10 1984057197
ISBN-13 978- 1984057198

PRESIDENT TRUMP HAS A <u>HUGE</u> FEAR
OF BEING POISONED. HE LOVES FAST FOOD
BECAUSE: "AT LEAST YOU KNOW
WHAT THEY ARE PUTTING IN IT."